This book is in the care of:

For my children,

May the wonders of God never fail to stir your souls and captivate your minds.

— Daddy

Seek First Productions, LLC - established 2012

Font style "storybook" created by Melissa Owens.

ISBN: 979-8-218-14022-9

Library of Congress Control Number: 2023901142

{Our God}

Where Does God Live?

by James M. Thayer
EDITED BY Aly Thayer

Seek First Productions, LLC | NASHVILLE, TN

God is omnipresent.

What in the world does that mean?!

That word doesn't have anything to do with **presents** (as in gifts)!

It means that God is <u>**EVERYWHERE**</u> at the same time.

He's there at the bottom of the Ocean.

He's there on the Moon.

God is with us...

When we eat breakfast in the morning.

He watches over us when we fall asleep at night.

Because God is omnipresent...
He's in heaven also!

In fact, heaven is God's throne. He's a Righteous King ruling from there. How neat!

When God's people lived outdoors (thousands of years ago!) they would meet with Him in a large tent called the Tabernacle.

Later, when they settled the land
God had promised them,

God's people built a beautiful temple
to honor and worship Him in!

If you're a follower of Jesus, God actually lives inside of you!

Your body becomes a temple for Him.

Worshiping at church is like a...

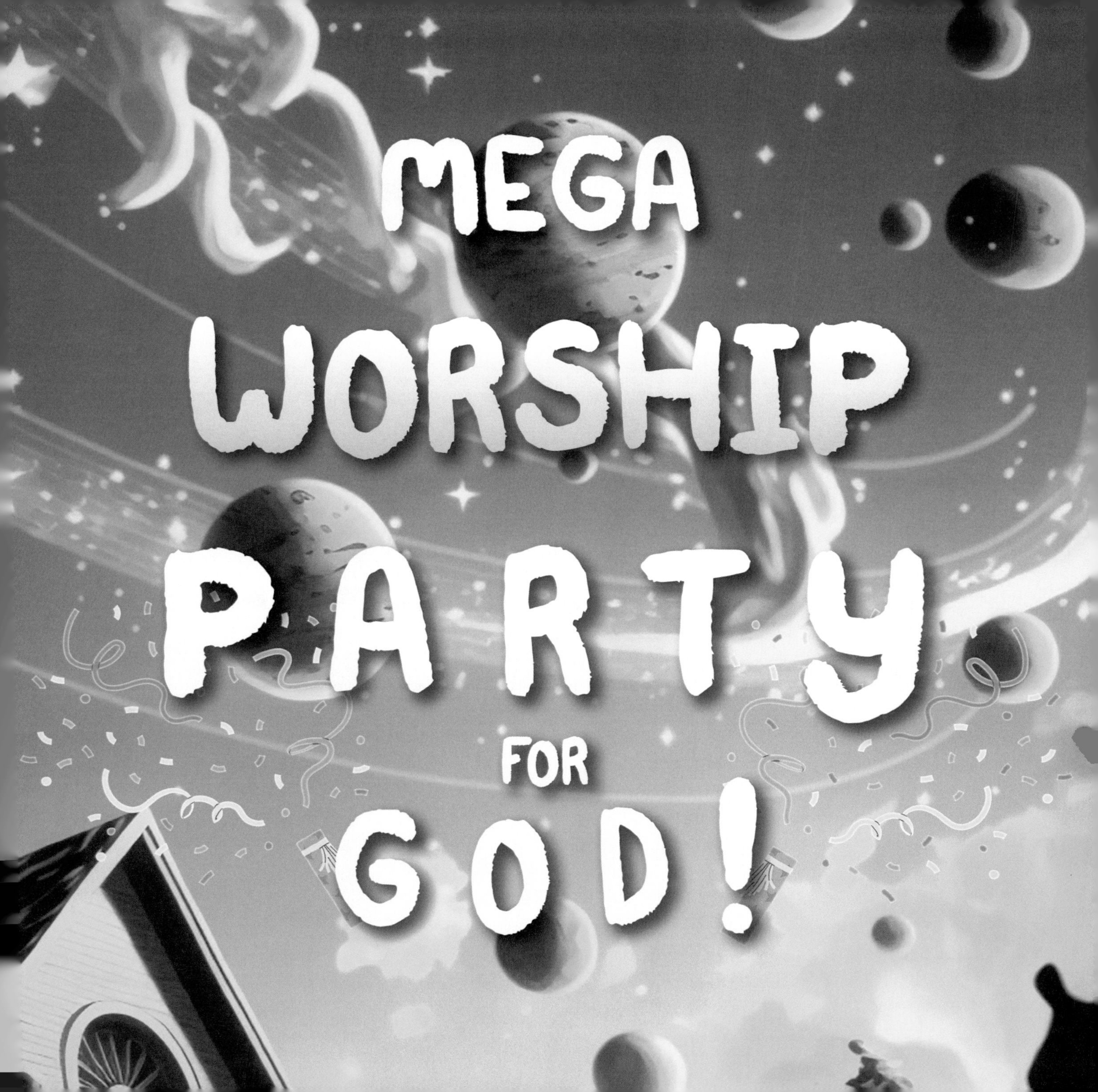
MEGA
WORSHIP
PARTY
FOR
GOD!

Church is also where we learn things about God, like His omnipresence, which helps us grow closer to Him and understand Him better.

"Where can I go from your Spirit? Or where can I flee from your presence?"
– Psalm 139

Well, let me ask you this – have you ever seen the wind?
Think
REALLY
hard!

I bet you've at least seen what the wind can do! Leaves blowing in the breeze, dust kicking up, and even snow or rain traveling sideways...

Can you think of some other things that you know are there even though they're invisible?

Things like...

GRAVITY!

We see it in action
whenever we throw a ball.

Sound...

We feel the effects of it when we're being

LOUD and SILLY!

Thoughts...

No one has ever seen a thought before, and yet all of the best inventions come from them!

and WIFI!

A movie can travel through the air from the internet to our smart phone (yeah, Science is THAT cool!)

Like all of these examples, God is
INVISIBLE

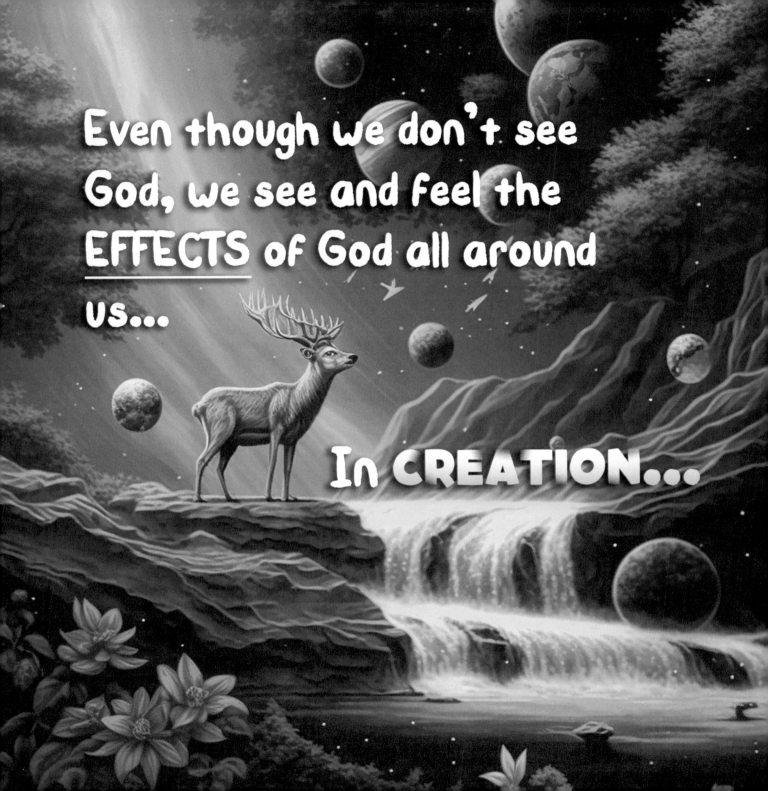

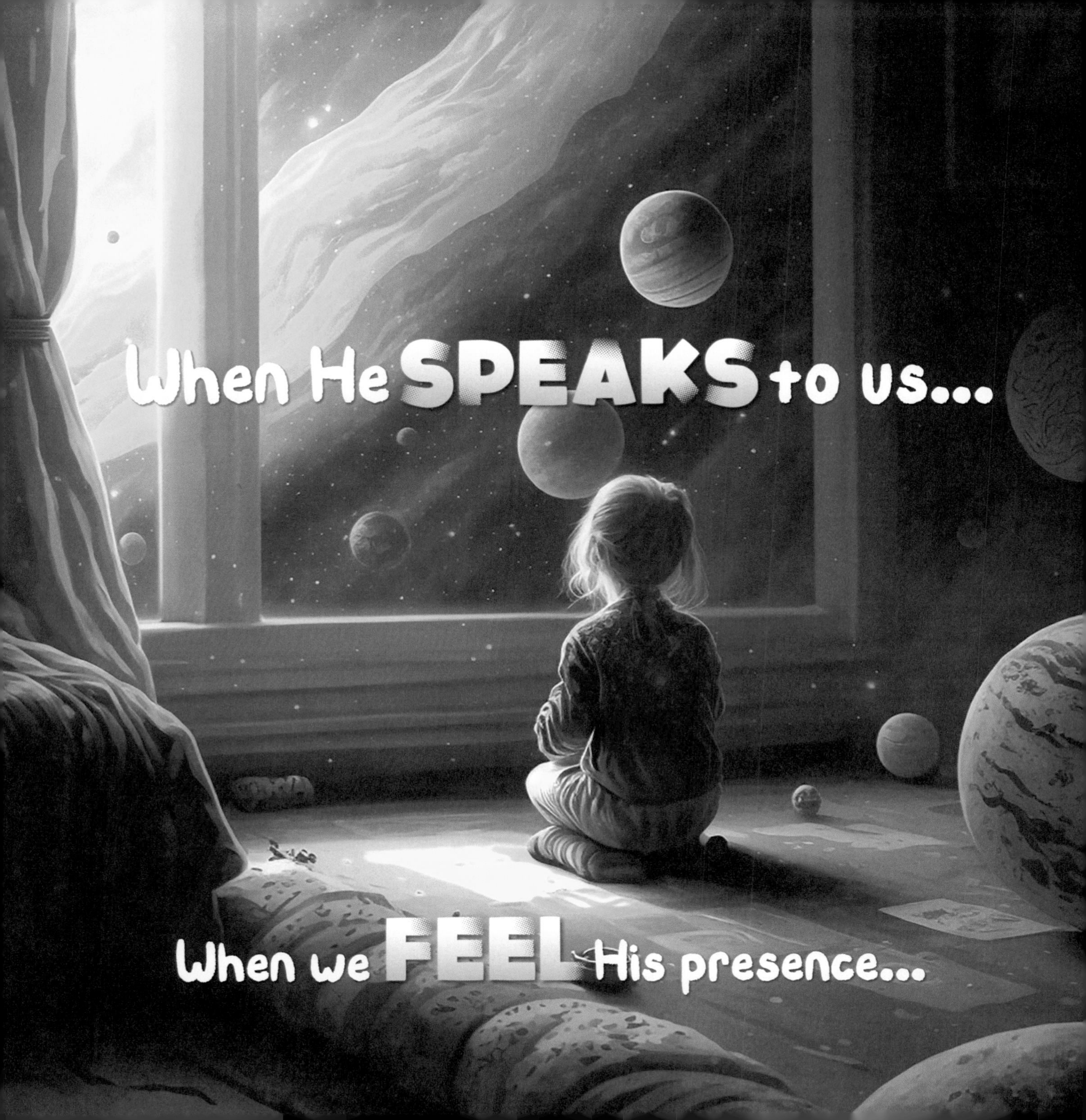

When He **SPEAKS** to us...

When we **FEEL** His presence...

When someone is **MIRACULOUSLY** healed...

And in ourselves when He **CHANGES** our hearts and minds.

Actually, YES! Since Jesus is God, when He walked on the Earth, everyone who saw Him saw God!

What made Jesus so special was His **DIVINITY**, which means He was God even though He was also a man.

Before Jesus went <u>back</u> to heaven, He told His friends,

"My Father's house has many rooms; Trust Me, I am going there to prepare a place for you!"

Questions for Discussion

1. Knowing that God is omnipresent, how might that affect us when we find ourselves in scary places or situations?

2. What do you think it will be like to live in God's house one day? Read Revelation 21 for more insight.

3. If God the Holy Spirit lives inside of you, how might that affect the way you interact with other people?

4. In the Old Testament of the bible, there was a large curtain in the Temple. Beyond this was the presence of God. What, then, do you think is the significance of Matthew 27:51?

Author's note:

So where does God live? God's presence is everywhere (He's omnipresent!) There is nowhere we can go where He won't be. Because of our sins, though (a topic for another book), we aren't in right relationship with Him. He is a personal God who desires relationship with His children (us!) It is only through Jesus that we can be have a good relationship with Him. If you follow Jesus, you will find God makes His home inside of you — and you'll never be the same again.

Glossary

Om·ni·pres·ent | (of God) Present everywhere at the same time

Tab·er·na·cle | A house of worship; A temporary shelter : TENT

Tem·ple | A building for religious practice

In·vis·i·ble | Incapable by nature of being seen; not perceptible by vision

Scripture Citations

"God is Omnipresent."
Jeremiah 23:24, 1 Kings 8:27, Colossians 1:17, Psalm 139:7-10, Job 34:21

"God's throne is in heaven, and He rules from there."
Psalm 11:4, Matthew 5:34, Matthew 23:22, Isaiah 66:1, Revelation 4:1-6, Psalm 103:19

"At one time God's people would meet with Him in the Tabernacle."
Exodus 40:2, Numbers 9:15, Acts 7:44, Exodus 33:9

"Later, a beautiful temple was created to worship God in."
2 Samuel 7:13, 1 Kings 5:5, 1 Kings 6:2, 1 Kings 8:11-13

"Now we no longer have to be in a certain place to experience God; our bodies are His temple."
John 4:21-24, 1 Corinthians 6:19-20, Romans 8:10, Galatians 2:20, Ephesians 3:17, John 14:16-18

"That doesn't mean we shouldn't go to church, though."
Hebrews 10:25, Acts 2:42

"Church is where we can learn things about God, such as His omnipresence."
2 Timothy 3:16-17

"God is invisible."
Colossians 1:15, 1 Timothy 1:17

"We see and feel the effects of God all around us."
Romans 1:20

"One of the miraculous things about Jesus is His divinity."
John 10:30

"When people saw Jesus, they saw God."
Colossians 1:15

"If we follow Jesus, we will see God with our eyes one day too."
Revelation 22:4

Before Jesus went to heaven, He told his friends, "My Father's house has many rooms; Trust me, I am going there to prepare a place for you!"
- John 14:2

Printed in the USA
CPSIA information can be obtained
at www.ICGtesting.com
LVRC080053020224
770677LV00009B/20